D0601393

I Have Feelings

CHILDREN'S SERIES ON PSYCHOLOGICALLY RELEVANT THEMES

Titles

by Joan Fassler
ALL ALONE WITH DADDY

THE MAN OF THE HOUSE

ONE LITTLE GIRL

MY GRANDPA DIED TODAY

THE BOY WITH A PROBLEM

DON'T WORRY, DEAR

by Terry Berger
I HAVE FEELINGS

I Have Feelings

by TERRY BERGER

Photographed by I. Howard Spivak

BEHAVIORAL PUBLICATIONS INC.

EARLY CHILDHOOD
EDUCATION PROJECT

Manufactured in the United States of America
Library of Congress Catalog Card Number

70-147123
SBN: 87705-021-X

Second printing November 1971

I am indebted to my son, David,
and to my sister, Sandra, who were more than
helpful. But above all, to Dr. Albert Ellis.

For everyone who has feelings.

I have feelings.

Some are good and some are bad, just like yours.

In the spring I plant some seeds and by the end
of the summer they have grown into juicy carrots.
My mother puts them in a salad.

I feel proud.

I weeded and watered the baby plants. That's why the carrots were so good. Working at something helps to make it happen.

Sometimes my brother teases me when we're having dinner. He keeps on calling me names.

I feel angry.

After a while I just stop listening to him and I
think about something else. Even if he keeps on saying
nasty things about me, that doesn't mean they're true.

I work on my model plane all morning but it keeps on falling apart. I wanted to fly it today.

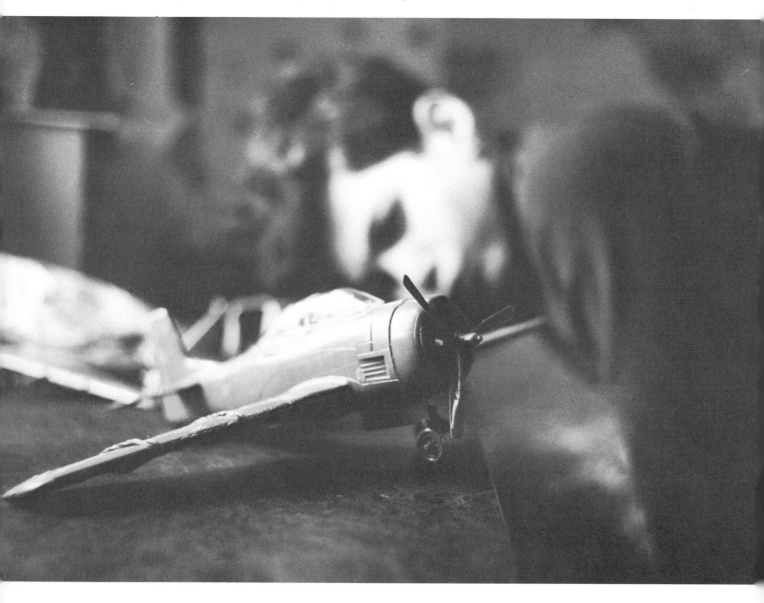

I feel disappointed.

When my mother comes into the room, I am crying.
She says that things can not always happen when you want
them to. It's too bad you can't change that but
you can get used to it.

Every Saturday my mother takes me shopping.
One time I show her a game that I really want.
She won't buy it for me.

I feel that my mother does not love me.

As we drive home, we talk and laugh. I know that my mother really cares for me. I didn't get the game, but nobody can get everything he wants.

My parents are out. I am wrestling with my brother
in the living room. I fall over and break my mother's new plant.

I feel I am bad.

My babysitter helps clean up. She says that doing something wrong does not mean I'm bad. It means that I made a mistake and I must be more careful.

Last Thursday I tried out for the ball team.
Only two boys didn't make it. I was one of them.

I felt like nothing.

My father and I walked to the park. He told me if I practiced
I would get better, but even so, not everyone can make the team.
You don't have to be the best to feel like something.

This week I try out for the school band.
I make it!

I feel good!

Now I'm glad I practiced every day even though I missed some ball games. Sometimes you have to give up something, to get something you want even more.

Jenny, the girl who sits next to me in school,
has pretty hair. I want to talk to her but I never do.

I feel shy.

Riding home on the bus, I think about her. Maybe she is shy too. I'll speak first and if she doesn't answer I can always talk to someone else.

The teacher calls on me. My answer is wrong.
All the children laugh at me.

I feel ashamed.

After school the teacher calls me to her desk.
She says that no one is always right.
Everybody makes mistakes sometimes.

On the way home from school, two boys start
bothering my friend. I help chase them away.

I feel brave.

Even though I may get hurt, I help my friend.
I must take a chance if I feel that I'm doing the right thing.

When I get home, Barry calls to tell me that he can't come over. I have no one to play with.

I feel lonely.

After a while I get a book and some toys.
I find that I can have fun when I am alone too.

During the holidays, Aunt Sandy comes to visit us.
She brings a big toy for my brother
and a little one for me.

I feel jealous.

I complain to my aunt.
She says there is no reason to bring us both the same things.
Just because she brings a bigger toy for my brother
doesn't mean she loves me any less.

One night while my aunt is still visiting our dog gets
so sick he can't play. He doesn't even eat his food.

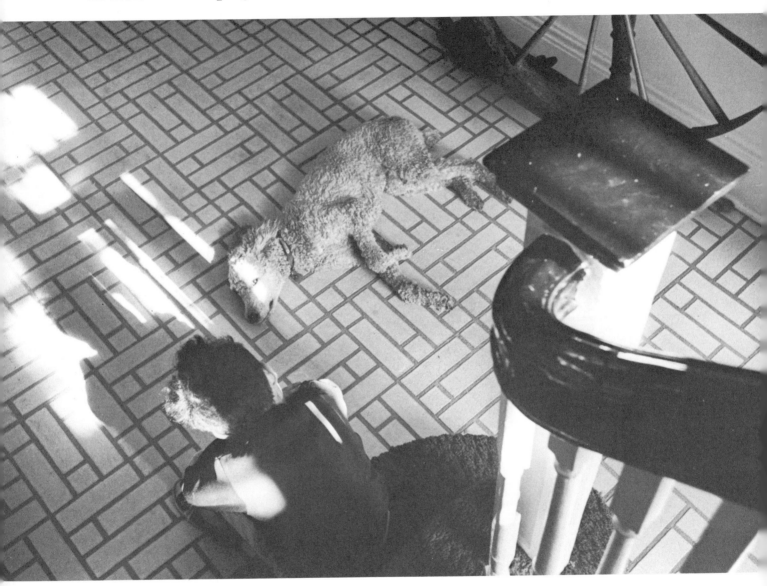

I feel sad.

We take our dog to the animal hospital
and I bring along his favorite toy.
If he dies I'll be very sad and I'll cry.
But dogs are like people and they have to die too.
Nobody can live forever.

The lady next door asks me to watch her baby.
She needs something from the store.

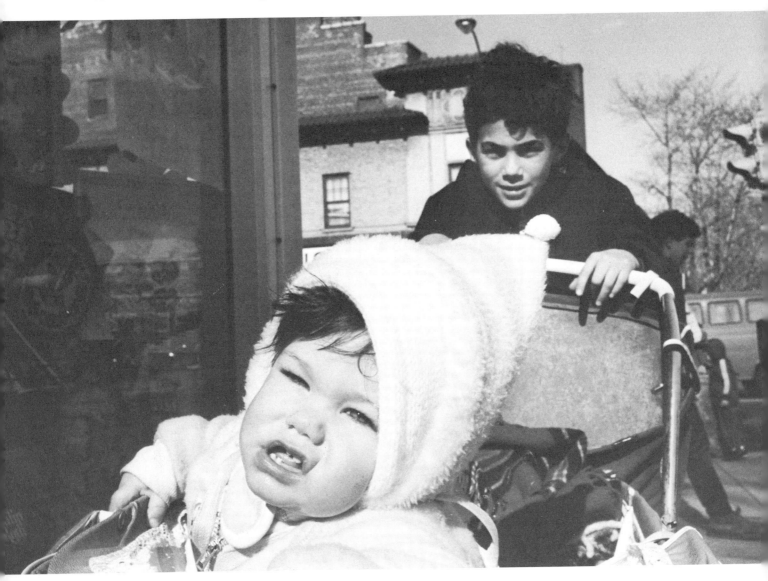

I feel important.

Rocking the baby to sleep I keep on thinking—
It's nice to know I can do the job.

Mark is having a party. David and Susan were invited.
I was not.

I feel left out.

I play with my turtle and I tell him that some people don't like me. But I don't like everybody either. Not being invited means that everyone can't like everybody else.

My mother and father are having a fight.
Will they make up?

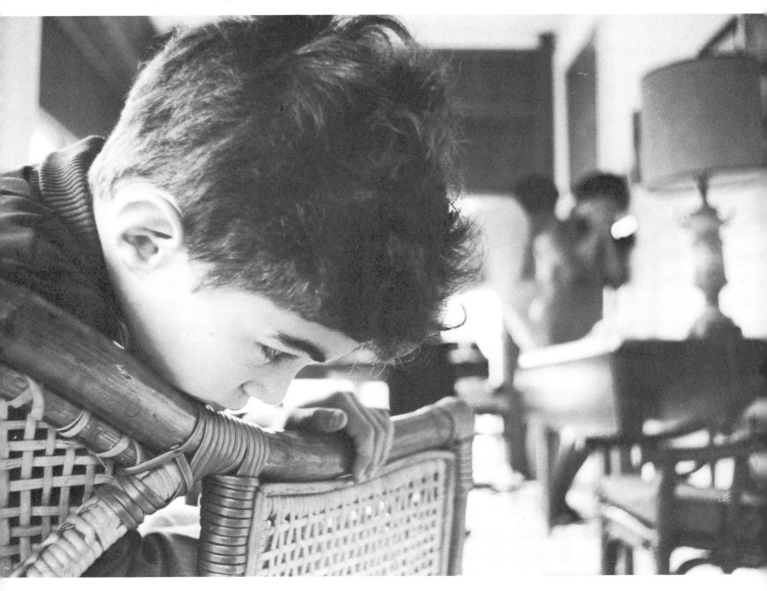

I feel frightened.

I run to my sister. She tells me not to worry. Our parents still love us, even if they can't get along sometimes.

It's Friday after school and I have no homework.
Soon I'll be going out with Jon, who's lots of fun.
We're going to ride our bikes.

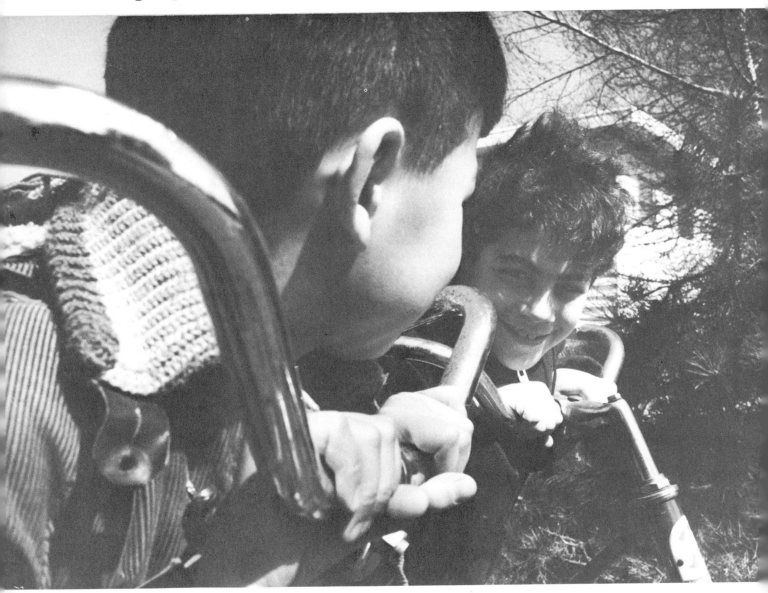

I feel happy.

I am happy when I do something I like.

I am happy when I'm with someone I like.

I am happy because I like myself.

The End